FAMOUS
ATHLETES

RUSSELL
WILSON

by Mari Schuh

Pebble
Plus

20

CAPSTONE PRESS
a capstone imprint

Pebble Plus is published by Capstone Press,
1710 Roe Crest Drive, North Mankato, Minnesota 56003
www.capstonepub.com

Library of Congress Cataloging-in-Publication Data
Cataloging-in-publication information is on file with the Library of Congress.

ISBN 978-14914-8510-1 (hardcover)
ISBN 978-14914-8530-9 (paperback)
ISBN 978-14914-8526-2 (eBook PDF)

Editorial Credits
Gina Kammer, editor; Heidi Thompson, designer; Eric Gohl, media researcher;
Lori Barbeau, production specialist

Photo Credits
AP Photo: Four Seam Images/Tony Farlow, 13, Richmond Times-Dispatch/Mark Gormus, 9;
Newscom: Cal Sport Media/Bill McGuire, 1, Icon SMI/Adam Davis, 15, Icon SMI/Ric Tapia, 17,
MCT/David Eulitt, 5, MCT/Ethan Hyman, 11, UPI/Jim Bryant, cover, UPI/John Angelillo, 19,
UPI/Kevin Dietsch, 21; Richmond Times-Dispatch: 7

Design Elements: Shutterstock

Note to Parents and Teachers

The Famous Athletes set supports national curriculum standards for social studies related to people, places, and culture. This book describes and illustrates Russell Wilson. The images support early readers in understanding the text. The repetition of words and phrases helps early readers learn new words. This book also introduces early readers to subject-specific vocabulary words, which are defined in the Glossary section. Early readers may need assistance to read some words and to use the Table of Contents, Glossary, Read More, Internet Sites, Critical Thinking Using the Common Core, and Index sections of the book.

Printed in the United States of America in North Mankato, Minnesota.
052016   009763R

TABLE OF CONTENTS

Football star Russell Wilson was born November 29, 1988. At age 5, Russell played football with his dad and older brother. Russell passed the ball to his brother.

1988

born in
Cincinnati, Ohio

Russell grew up

in Richmond, Virginia.

He was a star athlete

in high school.

He played baseball,

basketball, and football.

born in
Cincinnati, Ohio

Russell was a quarterback

in high school. He led the team

to state championships

in 2005 and 2006.

Russell also earned

all-state honors twice.

1988

2005 2006

born in
Cincinnati, Ohio

leads high
school football
team to state
championships

STAR ATHLETE

After high school Russell went to North
Carolina State University. He played
baseball and football. In three seasons,
Russell threw 76 touchdown passes.
It was the second-best in school history.

1988

2005,
2006

born in
Cincinnati, Ohio

leads high
school football
team to state
championships

In 2010 Russell was drafted

by the Colorado Rockies baseball team.

He played two seasons

in the minor leagues.

Russell played second base.

1988

born in
Cincinnati, Ohio

2005, 2006

leads high
school football
team to state
championships

2010

drafted by
Colorado Rockies
baseball team

13

In 2011 Russell played

his last year of college football

at the University of Wisconsin-Madison.

He led the team to a Big Ten title.

The team also played in the Rose Bowl.

1988

born in
Cincinnati, Ohio

2005,
2006

leads high
school football
team to state
championships

2010

drafted by
Colorado Rockies
baseball team

2011

leads the
Wisconsin Badgers
to a Big Ten title
and the Rose Bowl

Russell wearing number 16 for the Badgers

NFL QUARTERBACK

Many people thought Russell

was too short to be an NFL quarterback.

They were wrong. In 2012 Russell

became the quarterback

for the Seattle Seahawks.

NFL stands for National Football League.

1988
born in
Cincinnati, Ohio

2005 2006
leads high
school football
team to state
championships

2010
drafted by
Colorado Rockies
baseball team

2011
leads the
Wisconsin Badgers
to a Big Ten title
and the Rose Bowl

2012
starts to play
for the Seattle
Seahawks

Russell soon became an NFL star.

He was named the 2012 NFL Rookie of

the Year. In 2014 the Seahawks won

their first Super Bowl.

Russell threw two touchdowns.

1988
born in
Cincinnati, Ohio

2005, 2006
leads high
school football
team to state
championships

2010
drafted by
Colorado Rockies
baseball team

2011
leads the
Wisconsin Badgers
to a Big Ten title
and the Rose Bowl

2012
starts to play
for the Seattle
Seahawks

2014
leads Seahawks
to Super Bowl win

Russell led the Seahawks

to the Super Bowl again in 2015.

They lost the game. But Russell

wants to help the team win

many games in the future.

1988
born in
Cincinnati, Ohio

2005, 2006
leads high
school football
team to state
championships

2010
drafted by
Colorado Rockies
baseball team

2011
leads the
Wisconsin Badgers
to a Big Ten title
and the Rose Bowl

2012
starts to play
for the Seattle
Seahawks

2014
leads Seahawks
to Super Bowl win

2015
leads
Seahawks
to the
Super Bowl

GLOSSARY

Big Ten—a group of sports teams from different universities that play against each other

championship—a contest or tournament that decides which team is the best

draft—the process of choosing a person to join a sports organization or team

minor league—a league of teams where players improve their playing skills before joining a major league team

NFL—the National Football League

quarterback—a football player who leads the offense; quarterbacks pass the football or hand it off to a player

Rose Bowl—a college football game that is played every year; two of the top college football teams play in the Rose Bowl every January

Super Bowl—the final championship game in the NFL season

title—an award given to the winner of a tournament

touchdown—a six-point score in a football game

READ MORE

Appleby, Alex. *I Can Be a Football Player.* When I Grow Up. New York: Gareth Stevens Publishing, 2015.

Doeden, Matt. *All About Football.* All About Sports. North Mankato, Minn.: Capstone Press, 2015.

Lindeen, Mary. *Let's Play Football!* A Beginning to Read Book. Chicago: Norwood House Press, 2015.

INTERNET SITES

FactHound offers a safe, fun way to find Internet sites related to this book. All of the sites on FactHound have been researched by our staff.

Here's all you do:

Visit *www.facthound.com*

Type in this code: 9781491485101

Super-cool stuff! Check out projects, games and lots more at **www.capstonekids.com**

CRITICAL THINKING USING THE COMMON CORE

1. Some people thought Russell wouldn't become an NFL quarterback. Why did they feel this way? (Integration of Knowledge and Ideas)

2. How did Russell's family help him with sports when he was younger? Why might this be important as he grew up? (Integration of Knowledge and Ideas)

3. Name an award that Russell has won. Why was he given this award? (Key Ideas and Details)

INDEX